FLOATING HARBOUR

Tony D'Agrio

Herman Bowker

Stu

Frank Drake

To Caroline

FLOATING HARBOUR

Tony D'Arpino

photographs
Stephen Morris

First published in 2011 by Redcliffe Press Ltd., 81g Pembroke Road, Bristol BS8 3EA

www.redcliffepress.co.uk
info@redcliffepress.co.uk

© Tony D'Arpino, photographs © Stephen Morris

ISBN 978-1-906593-87-2

British Library Cataloguing-in-Publication Data
A catalogue record for this book is available from the British Library

Design and photography: Stephen Morris www.stephen-morris.co.uk
Printed in the Czech Republic via Akcent Media

CONTENTS

No use singing, it seems to me,
unless the song comes from the heart,
and song cannot come from the heart
unless true love is there already.

Bernart de Ventadorn

Seahenge

from Osip Mandelstam

We do not need the island's gifts,
A forest of uninvited ships.

Nature's the same as Rome, was reflected in it.
We see images of its civic might
In the clear air and sky-blue circus,
In the forum of fields, the colonnades of groves.

I swung in a distant garden
On a plain wooden swing,
Tall dark trees
In a feverish haze.

A flame is in my blood
Burning dry life to the bone.
I do not sing of stone,
Now I sing of wood.

Light and rough wood
Made of a single spar,
The oak's deep heart
And the fisherman's oar.

Drive them deep the harbour piles,
Hammer them in tight
Around the wooden paradise
Where everything is light.

Night in the Apple Orchard

the girls glow
like precious jewels

they are themselves
a source of light

brightening
the summer darkness

I think and see
a dream country

of magic mud
and apple sky

the floating stars
lotus flowers

blue ponies waiting
in the trees

Chatterton

I thought of Chatterton again today
the boy poet of my new home town
and other boy poets I have known
they were young men of course no longer boys
but pretty and intense and not really crazy
toying with the ancient and new ways of seeing

five seasons now I've passed his house
(his uncle the sexton of St Mary Redcliffe)
and I find the house is not as old as I expect
it's the parchment forgeries of the old monk
a handful of centuries confused and hypertexted
that flicker in my mind's back-lot book of days

contemporaries of the atmosphere of heaven
walking the mazy lanes eyelids in romantic movement
a long line unrolling from the inner ink well
later in the anthems we were the mods of Main Street
dressed like troubadours with electric combs
memory is the love song of eternity

From the Forest of Avon

I'm the tree and the door
in the basement of the book
you didn't read that night
that day in the dark
where the paraffin
translated the loft
into the penmanship of water

I dreamed the dresser
put cuff links on me
gold or bright bone links
on my blue shirt
my wrists hidden in a fat river
my ceiling a splinter of wood
I fly now to the treetops

the sky is an egg
inside outside
the nest
the dark woods
blackbird hidden
in the tree of the fence
the language retranslating itself

I do not hammer these trees
together for echo's sake but
for the water coursing through them
these trees are my moat
square circle of living ramparts
my night and my map
a path for stars

Bristol Bridge

the kids in Bristol are sharp as a pistol
when they do the Bristol stomp
and once you dance with me
you'll fall in love you see

The Dovells, *Bristol Stomp*

a forest of maps and folding masts
our ships sail under the bridge
some say the bridge was a fortress
some say the bridge is the town

like handprints in the water
nobody knows when the bridge was built
the sculpture of a dancing river
a catalogue of ships

our gabled double world seeing up and
down and twice a day the memory
one enters the city by water
another enters by the bridge

songs known all over the city
a harbour of signs and weirs
while I wander in the woods
downtown again a forest

the curving arches
the flowing through
of the seven-storey bridge
great shells of the ocean turtle

ending in the blue
clear day in February
centuries later or now
here in boots

and loud above the Bristol stomp
the high clear scream of the gulls
frozen on the bridge
the happiest man in the world

as the power of a single tree
can dominate the forest
so a single bridge
can change the course of history

river goddess dancing girl
the floating harbour
a bridge of air
above the floating world

Buñuel vs Brunel

four cranes
with the steeple beyond
cathedrals of voyages

and the darkness
of some post holes in Wiltshire
old tugboats moored in a glade of cranes

across the harbour from the Grove
thinking upriver past Conham Ferry
owls hush the floating woods

near the love tunnel of cranes
the C-curve of the steam crane
brontosaurus framing dark water
where the invisible circus dancer
rehearsed on the mid-air hook
before the first morning ferry
like alpha bridge at night
a parabola of light like oars
suspended in cuckoo spit

dear skull shall it be
Nympfo & Lenzman
Tonite at the Thekla

death grinning
his stencil tag
at the waterline

my river of wind
south of the real
the other land's end   29 30 31 32

The Mute Swans at Welsh Back

the Pisan tilt of the Llandoger Trow
shadows the beer and lends
medieval lines to the old neighbourhood

nearby the needle of St Mary Redcliffe
more tapered than Cleopatra's
but from the same warren

stands noonish in a mesh
of rivers and birds
and circling hares

tap tap tap blind Pew
the black spot grows like the lichen
on the tables of Shakespeare's brown October

the leaning church of the Templars
circular temple
invisible circles now

rusting bollards
from every era
line the loud docks

swans mute swans   mute swans mute
here and in the New Cut   only on the water
beyond the gate of the ruined prison   when they fly

where the tidal wash   they bleat a little
becalms   with each wing
the low tide mute button   beat mute swans sing

The Music of Five Oceans

water is an island
covered in maps

sky sovereign
the sea quick

yet polished
like her pebbles

a creature passing
a nest of beaches

south
to the changing names

looking up
through a column of mayflies

a pale jet
passes in the blue

and a wedge of geese
fly into the paper

they fly both ways
in black and white

the south wind
brings the island to the island

the sea starts at the hedgerow
the horizon falls out of your eye

in the magic gardens of Clifton Vale
a memory quivers in the heart of time

and a muse of water offers ballast flora
the long poem of the old docks

first syllable of accented west
the lazy contralto of the blackbirds

the colour of the lunar hare
racing across the waves

the river is a dirty goddess
winking at the boys

playing in the sun
the river is a dancing goddess

five foxes on the downs
in the late afternoon

green bush cricket
in the wood pile

three pines
in the car park at Stonehenge

a long street full of ships
a long lake full of suns

a dream remembered
in a dream

the colours of memory
wash the long now

the Half King
narrowboat visitor

moored at the end or beginning
of St Augustine's Reach

ships lying in the ooze afloat
when the river was amphora

the sloes a blue galaxy
in a sea of green leaves

bright amber evening
outside the Nova

among the spiderwebs of rigging
a language knife

picture container
siege-engine of wind

swans like white kanji
moving on the dark floating basin

in Hoefnagle's map of Bristol 1573
from the atlas *Civitates Orbis Terrarum*

the castle and its moat
is the eye of the engraving

in Millerd's map of Bristol 1673
the castle is gone

clouds reflected in the river
the water kiln

two peregrine falcons
playing in the gorge

cloud bones
of mackerel sky

Rancocas red
silver river skin

a young girl dancing
in electric blue moccasins

pine cone full moon
a chorus of gifts

the sky looks ocean today
vast deeps and tower drops

above the bands of sea
the green and blue

below lagoons
of deeper channels

celtic words like rocks
lost anchors new found lands

the petrified clam
by the garden door

old succulent mollusc
heavy with time

a stream that wraps
around her stone

yet glimmers
with streaks of day

the sand that flows
through the belly

turtle hourglass
holding the world

To Phoenix Wharf

a long low sigh
motorcycle
along the Grove
across the light

the wharf in all its burning bird
and sunset shades
the evening carving
the morning

the old drawbridge screams
and echoes back St Augustine's Reach
what is a bridge after all
in a gull's world

at Temple Meads
where the sun was once
a vast grey pewter
egg of dawn

the bells of St Mary Redcliffe
change ringing for two hours of rehearsal
above the poet shed
the voice of mud and water

now a great plate of sun
in Bathhurst Basin
blasts upon The Ostrich
her bath of light

drowned by the bells
and punctuated by the boom
of black powder quarter hour
cannon from the *Matthew*

a day of winds
bagpipes inventing
the sound of barking dogs
from the black barge

like the carillons of Coleridge
at Ottery St Mary
peeling seven hours at a time
the wheat fields bright with fire

Daruma

By the time I painted the second eye
You had already changed
Into a forest

Daruma lucky household god
Part hedgehog monkey doll
Rabbit of the moon

God of toys and politics
Like a garden stone that speaks
Fairies don't grant wishes

They make decisions
I decided to wish for someone
Who could imagine this

Chalk

ancient colours
new thoughts

a woman on the legs
of a horse

a centauress
appearing suddenly

in the village green
white horse heat

a horse
of three white lines

a tail an eye
a flank

facing the sky

If April

the light
on the rosebuds
is a steady light

in changeable air
fashioned from the warmth
of the harbourmaster's hut

the light reflects
off the floating harbour
and the local network

of water and quays
to the channel
and the ocean of dreams

the light
of my image
resembles clear words

but they are not words
green brown blue
earths

if april
one word
one wood

Moondog

Gibbous this twilight
Going full with a shady rainbow

The edges of the Avon
Lashed with filigree plate

Inverted bowl of the downs
Wet edge facing Bristol

Mud glowing white
At the foot of the gorge

A canopy of local skin
Above the hidden hot springs

Still flowing below the surface
Of the river and reflected light

Tree Horse

the bird-like entity
between pegasus
and the trekking orpheus

is a talisman
the v-shape tree
of the orphanage

and the rabbit hut
behind the old hospital
near an ancient osage orange

tell me
the sand dunes
beyond

mix
with feral bombs
the rocks transforming

into arrival
moss man
on the bridle path

The Yellow Snail

a tiny orb
spiral spinning
not slo mo
but eyeball sky

you in the turret
above the lot
my idea is dancing
in the smoky garden

a perfect yellow spiral
rabbit knowledge
a perfect dance
in all the natural colours

and pasta pie
Mississippi recipe
from a charred
and flooded book

orthography of spiral
flourish of rain water
on the unpainted boards
above the bricks

Rosewood

in hedgerow
the city streets are born
they carry my carve

my song
and my fence
the yurt that folds

into the pocketbook
accordion of maps
rose of teleportation

a magic car
made of tiny arrows
a music of curling roads

where jazz and stone
face the old forest
in the flesh

beech thighs
skin of my sky
red tiles under blue

the traveller mirrors the wheels
spice rack of the wind
in a vestibule of red

red box of my heart
red path to the woods
my hand in all her plumage

Lapin Chaud

rabbit nose gleaming
in deep forest sky
white clouds sliding
down the glass day
high jump of gate
delayed for one last

kiss

before the mist develops
a daguerreotype of lanes
and rabbit warrens winding
toward the footbridge lens
the town made of willow stone
reeds and white fur clouds

Oak and Elephant

in the oaks I dream of elephants
and you in the heart of palms
my forest lover shade and light
in you I hold the forests of my hand
the herds of ancient memories
future trees above the air
and envelopes of green succession
I remember this and forget the dreams
of the night before and the islands
of our future appear like clouds
on the horizon of our double sea

The Floating Harbour

neptune floats
at temple meads
watching over
the mapmaker's daughter

brown virgo eyes
that see the world in its full blue
and the green man from jersey
strolling in from a tree ship

with roses from woodhenge

To an English Garden

of sky

enchantment
a place
where snails slide
on ribbons of time
a place of drowsy bees
and blackbirds

snogging flowers

speaking letters in a door
along a road of colour
fences speaking brightness
dreaming
in another language
conjugating

time zones

my midnight
is your morning
our time a ribbon
connecting continents
unwrapped like a gift
in a visible package

of sky

Memory Bird

nuts scatter in the great room
the tower remembers every turn
pine nuts scissored from the cones
a forest calendar on the forest floor
flash of bird colour and bluestone
a mirror roosting in a notch of beechwood
tiny birds in wind-combed cypress

a list of trees and a dinosaur
then I remember going with Moo
to see Pharaoh Sanders at the Savoy Tivoli
that language lifting trees into the sky
and the buzzing of big red bumblebees
a sound imitated by memory
windward unhurried but sure

are you birch enough
to bend
in white grey rain
same day

are you balloon enough
to trap the wind
and sin
in faithful tango

are you bird enough
to fly above
the harbour
seeing not the clay

are you light
enough
and gate enough
for the bird

but the lay of the near meridian

of the open book

Vision at Vauxhall Footbridge

the same solitude at the end
of each marina pier the dash
between the land
and my water camp
where souls begin to see
to dream

tapas and stained glass
I'm glad I wrote the voices
in our bright envelopes of gas
mirror mandala
double spiral
black pearl necklace

carib
laughter and unshed tears
or the White Horse Tavern
voting with Poe
or Labour In Vain
Clare's lost pub

colours like the molten language
of the glass-blower's art
two balloons in a day moondog
a perfect circle around the sun
a goddess married to a sword
a goddess married to a banana tree

Underfall Yard

hello my lover it's special
to have dreams of poetry
thin blue volumes
bound in red Tibetan wax

the Bristol Channel a forest of mud
the voice from the south
a butterfly battery
cleaning the Gulf Stream

the joy of rocking on
the floating island
in the under bridge
overflow of light

suspended in the gorge
of a true sister of shade
the swan keeper's ferry
crossing the light

a liquid book
in map-time nap time
a labyrinth of lacquer
crying salmon dreams

Blackbird

To Gwen

you know what you want
and you are what you need

gliding from flower to sky
a background of blue

foregrounded in music the stroller forgot
I step in the lane to remember

I know who you are
like a voice in a name

Song of the Water Man

for Jim Karnstedt

begin in air
near the waterfall
then leave the land of lakes

and never fish again
except for a glint of motorcycle chrome
and tropes of light in the water

and good day
you have reached the long pole
of the punt across the river ion

the network extends
across the fields of welcome
we are the waters of your memory

St Mary Redcliffe

from Hölderlin

Like a stamen inside a flower
The steeple stands in lovely blue
And the day unfolds around its needle

The flock of swallows that circles the steeple
Flies there each day through the same blue air
That carries their cries from me to you

We know how high the sun is now
As long as the roof of the steeple glows

Great Western

I'm not the person I was
And I'm not the person I'm becoming
I'm not the person I am
Because of the language

Of the yellow and the blue
I'm the language of colour
And the allotment of you
I'm not a flower

In the small real garden
The magic blackbird sings
In the middle of the tree
One unknown dreamer

I'm sitting with the bird in the tree
And I can see the invisible castle
From the bridge the others can't see
Not far from the train station

Transported

how quickly we understood the trees
when botany bay was a prison of flowers
we called new woods

tree window river
dream fins our eyes
the cave called us dawn

the natural history of paths
lightning (weeping) strikes
paper trees

banked rivers
window parts
annealing in the woods

who are the words and dreams
names assigned
to parts of speech

it's us
the shadow club
white silk

we heard the story
built a simple fort
each one of us

became a tree

John Clare's Badger

Where are the animals in poetry?
Yes yes some birds in bushes and trees
But where are the teeming sub-continents

The papery nests of wild bees
Urban animals
The raccoon god of Shinto
The homely rat
Tiny dinosaurs of desire
And birds of appetite

John Clare's badger
Tamed squirrels
And feral pigeons
The house cat and fly
Curious dogs
Quiet spiders
Domestic vermin

Darting back
Through the dogs and rings
A growling badger
Escapes
Slipping through the legs
Of the village idiot
John Barleycorn
Reborn

Postcard from the Coast of Bohemia

for Simon

Waking up in Dr Dee's
Old apartment in Prague

A stuffed two-headed calf
Is watching us from his perch

Near the alchemical library movie screen
The scrying glass between the windows

Alive with the motes of morning
The best beach in Bohemia

Is just around the corner
From the astronomical clock

And if you say Orloj you will learn
The location of the secret rave

One August

loves August
augurs two

rain sun night
moon two days

the you me harbour
two rivers

two days later
on the Via della Botteghe Oscure

cicadas crying dawn
four temples

the secret forest
bristle of wet hair

on a neon rooftop
in Trastevere

my brother jokes
tell her you love her

noon underground   fills my hair with smoke
a feast of blue   night clouds

in Rome   parting for the moon
your scent   a full fresh rose of garlic

At the Source of the Avon

all my dreams
wrapped in stars

you are my local
specific landscape

now green now isle
from which forever is composed

the silk route of your arm
in the fire light

a path of blue chiselled by the wind
in the moving marble of clouds

the kind of day love poems
appear on all the café tables

lines written and left
in the spill of the road

a rhyming dictionary
left on a chair in the sun

beech leaves fill the mattress
of the talking bed

Corfe Castle Revisited

hair curly like the ocean
we stand on the cliff
pagan map waving in the wind

your gift is my world
our gifting mutual map
wrapped in sky

our kind of travelling
is nomadic staying
our road of the winds

and a still point
memory map
three words

located
in birdsong
what can be said

in the fields
running in the grass
shout of clouds

in the shingle far below
the salt
singing in the sand

Blue Gate, Blue Door

I knew the number of your gate
And the music of the hidden garden door
Before I saw or heard the braking trains
At Temple Meads

Nine
Surrounded by the muses of one blue
Summertide
The hottest summer since the troubadours

Sings in the same key of cicada
Heard along the Tiber or the apple forests
Of Asia Minor and the South
Sings as well as any oak

Blue
Travels through our maps
The restless breeze flipping pages
Of an atlas left by the garden door

Radio Caroline

The Irish pirates sing a coast into view
The airwaves expanding like salt in the rain

The surf curls back to the duvet shore
The fish nuzzling up the spiral jetty

To the red and white lighthouse
Their fervent O's keening

Against the scalloped surface
A day-mark tango against the sky

Broadcasting maypole dancers
No sonar bouncing off May Hill

Bristol Byzantine answering the gulls
The soul of the cellar is rock and roll

Granary now music now oysters
Warehouse of smoke

Islands made of time
And space a tamer spice

In the evening of her eyes
Mixed with solitudes of noon

The wind sings in her hair
Radio radio Caroline

Forest Geometry

Silence has no end; speech is
just the beginning of it.
Thoreau

the path into the woods
cannot be seen from the treetops
the wind leads to another sky

the path follows roots
triangles of growth and fall
cradle of understory

the old book fell apart in my hands
near the kitchen garden the musty library smell
mingled with the herbs and mints

what seemed planet now a tragic sun
an archaeology of stars
excited in a new forest

the light sounds like someone
saying dream dream
in the gentle voice of a child

Ink Oak

all that it is to be human
can be seen in wood
Roger Deakin

pollen-rain
on the acorns
toll bridge way-bread

the duir the round oak
concentric logs of air
ink & gall of moving fluids

a hundred feet above the river
treehouse of the mind
the need-fire

using the tree as a pencil
I fly over the landscape
to the treehouse dark with smoke

stone acorns
tokens of the sacred oaks
in the next valley

the man with the mask of a pheasant
sips wine from a straw
clown laughter of gulls

green man
new ancient welcome
a book of water

swim swim
rain water-dancing
over Leigh Woods

in a book of trees
on knees of burr
word-thin wood of the glade

Balloons

A hot air balloon
with my name on it is out
of sight now heading to the Dundry Hills
having passed over the famous trees and spires
of Bristol balloons on the wet eyelids of morning
balloons filled with words and speaking dark toons
a moving collage of countryside & hedgerow curves
the wildwoods below like a decoupage of summer
fields the willow gondola is long enough for tango
lessons the old victrola gramaphone is brought
along with a picnic hamper itself a miniature
gondola microcosm of the sky and clouds
tiny fast moving forests of Avon agogo
balloons again in the afternoon
multi-coloured periplums
hanging up-side
down like a
good
hippie
or
bad
bus

written

inventions of the wind chime
hanging inside the air-earth
emblem of the fire-burner

Canzone Avalon

apple
soft vowel
open mouth

of the mists
tomato
of the tongue

the floating harbour
a flower in the mind
aquatint of sky reversed

a möbius murmuration
of starlings
over the downs

green star
sister of water and light
the earth floats free of the net

pears from france
and fair trade bananas
shipshape and bristol-stowed

in the belly of the city
world-maker
mud guardian

The Bird Studio

for Jane Furness

light green
from a dark palette
in a bright bird

like a long dream
squeezed out
of a single word

like a child
scolding a flower
the colours have a universe

the bird sings a transparent song
his honeycombed beak
like a rudder of light

a song
at the very tip
of feathered fingers

Sea Walls

a safe harbour
statement
you may have missed
in the tropic tumble

please wait a moment while
the magic starts up for the first time
behind Portishead Point
waiting in King Road for the wind

please wait please wait
consult the periplum
then the tide takes us in
all the way to Broad Quay

if a flower can hallucinate
describe

Yellow Spider

Ancient bones
Hiding in the flower
Disguised as the yellow centre
Of a purple star

Swaying spooky
In a wind of webs
The autumn flourish
Cloud nebula

Crowded with gold
And prehistoric eyes
An old sardine
Of alpha memory

Pale yellow pal
Without a web
My cunning crab
In forest flower

Dove Map

your velvet eyes
are my memory of the present
my now of sky and river bank

two cormorants again
at the end of the sea scouts' pier
disguised as their reflection

there must be fish after all
in this giant lock
dream fish for an ocean tribe

your velvet eyes
are my book of days
my now of sky

Bristol Allotment Onions

sweet yellow earth stars
glass cathedrals of the dirt

now drying in the sun
the same sun that warmed

the onion screw peeling wagon
at Uncle Joe's farm

onions braided
yellow and red

that first sweet bite
of angel flesh

o onions
onions

if all our food
is composed of souls

these tangy
paper-covered

puzzle-sweets
are feasts

On the Economy of the Universe

very very very
large sun of stone
the dirt king soars
above the market
autumn spring or summer

arms of gold
holding the candle wax
the altar cloth a mask in daylight
love's body
glowing in the singer's mouth

a stone cutter
leaves the church
a poor-box
illustrated history
of the rose window

tent of miracles
sea of roses
yap island coin
house of stars
tent of wheels

the great rose
glowing in the dark
cathedral
a wheel
of excess radiation

very very very
long stone of the sun
stones made holy
by geology
resting in the dark

cameras and songs
orbit the altar
a litany
in the lungs
of space

a perfect fuel
seeking a more perfect
transaction
the glowing
red star of our molten core

An Atlas for Orpheus

when her science bares her belly in a great room of birds
and her breasts are the two worlds I am familiar with

all her missing maps reassemble in the atlas of my eyes
and the island is a tunnel through the colour of the birds

rich dirt of hell the soil of our flowerbeds
speaking vegetables tumble from mother's open book

the other scrapbooks rot and dream themselves
back into the windows of our looking dream

Sons of Autumn

dessicated

leaf

a see-through

dirty angel wing

delicate

as feather absence

so close to the equinox

so far

from the stones

and lace

flutter of nothingness

a leaf of white blossom

now fallen now

draped over twig

melting like gold

leaf over twig

soft taking its form

becoming foam again

Durian Fruit

The Proas of Guam could fly 25 knots or more
Word pirate William Dampier logged their speed

The ships' naked skin celestial articles of voyage
As white as milk as soft as cream

Their putrid smell like roasted onions
When the durian falls the sarongs rise

Juan Fernandez says careen the Bachelor
Near pungent forests of sandalwood

And shiney-leafed pimento trees
The stormy petrel not unlike a sparrow

And a pretty little feathered creature
No bigger than a great overgrown wasp

With a black bill no bigger than a needle
Sailing in the flowers of the durian tree

Stanton Drew

the standing stones move like sheep
and distant trees
describe the first horizon
the summer soul

full moon mice
calendar bones
clouds passing
like a book of shadows

hedgehog
in a cloud of putty
the same solitude of thoughts
and pictures

the moon's zodiac
when silence
is a word
and everything is water

ghost sky
cloud towers
the sea itself
a bridge

Scipio

yes I'm Scipio
no doors to my tomb
maybe semi-sealed
like the entrance to the honeycomb

bees of the goddess
browse in the garden
they'll sting you to death
but they're not really bad

nonspecific coronas
orbiting the flowers
in a language unlike
these words of sand

for if men are ruled by words
which words offer freedom
and if men are ruled by dreams
which dreams are visions

these are the words and visions
I have sought in the vast body
of the sea and the desert land
and from the woman of the star map

I stopped and asked at my tomb
there were some travellers there
they knew some funny proverbs
but had nothing for the sand man

so I went onward into my wheel of wind
my body of rags and silk rivers
where geography becomes poetry
and each grain of sand is a star

To Gwen in February

1
I like how the sky
spells your name
when I'm not thinking

and I look up
and you're my world

2
shadow of eyelash

3
today the forests
stretch away
in the echo of your eye

4
the river
love-child
of the forest

5
the wind in the trees
never ruffles the swaying nest

6
what happened on that day
more than the hope
of trees and wind

a song

7
two badgers
in moonlight

8
the wind in the trees
is a cherished music

leafy branches
reaching
to their season

9
angel element
of the colour lithograph
periodic map of my world

you are my first
moving picture

10
a bird
moving word

11
my treasure
island girl

12
postcards
from the heart
like feathers of hope

on the deep forest
path

13
white

14
green

15
the like game

16
the river merchant
watches
the floating lanterns

17
from the edge
of the cliffs
to the bright tapers
in a fireplace

love gathers
in a few words

18
dark ink

19
illuminated prow

20
rain
music
a landscape

21
flame shoulder
willow beauty

22
a cresting wave
my pencil
made of incense

late post
new lark

23
retinal poetry

24
the light pours through
the upper eyelash

25
all my mothers
and fathers

seem reflected
in this water
where we watch

26
a moat of the moment

27
darling sky

Acknowledgements

An Atlas for Orpheus,
Flarestack Anthology (Birmingham)

Blue Gate, Blue Door, *Poetry Monthly* (Nottingham)

Daruma, *Barrow Street* (New York)

Forest Geometry, *Agenda* (Mayfield, East Sussex)
and *Poetry East* (DePaul University, Chicago)

John Clare's Badger, *The West Wind Review*
(Oregon State University, Ashland, Oregon)

Moondog and The Floating Harbour,
Suspension Magazine (Bristol)

On the Economy of the Universe,
Manchester Cathedral Anthology 2009
(Manchester)

Scipio appeared in the collection *Greatest Hits*,
Pudding House Publications (Columbus, Ohio)

Special thanks to Amanda Duke-Woolley
for gracious time and space in the land of the troubadours

and to Nicholas Campion and Wendy Buonaventura
for the star-dance of love and inspiration

and to Simon Bowler and Chris Hughes
for a yeoman's night tour of Bristol

and to Lee Bradley for close readings and 'the code'.

Bristol Castle

stonehenge in the family
the maps of the navigator
blowing from the caravans
like banners of the troubadours
your hair taming the wind
above the castle while the ponies
ate the apples we left at the camp

Apotheosis of Cuckoo Spit

The sound the white foam makes
Is the bird dream after-sound

Come to me in a sound
Soundlessly but with plenty coo

The mild double west
Marking stencils in the mind

A flourish of cartoons
And exotic weeds

The café wall illusion vibrating
At the foot of St Michael's Hill

The back lanes full of buddleia
And red valerian

We fix the cuckoo clock
And ship it home

Then under the corn-temple clock
You know the one with three hands

We have a coffee on the nails
Bright sundials of trade

Mells

a morning mile
maze of hawthorn
measured in scent
from the village of Mells

ancient paths
flower to flower
love to love

four oaks divide
and steal the scene
from the Luytens yew path
the wind piano

an old man carries flowers
through the churchyard
emanations

at night
a single owl
encourages the faceless clock
to sing a bell

a trout flops
through the surface
of the mill pond

the iron mills lost
in the dark of the River Mells
and the River Frome
modern ruins in forest time

mill architecture
now a watermark just visible
dream wood

iron stone
the cooling stream
under greenwoods
the English cathedral of paths

field sheep move slowly
in the tythe-mural
above the barman at the Talbot Inn

coloured leaves
spin
slant
scatter across the blue

beyond the hay-chapel
of the old walled garden
the glasshouse dances in the cold

autumn enters the mural
winter is personal
then spring explodes
beyond the edges of the mural wall

the tythe-barn a summer world
made of light
and the mays of Mells

The Bandage

Such a blunder
To cut my finger
With the new French knife

Because I need all my fingers to touch you

I touch the bandage to my skin then
Touch you
Deep surface of my world

The bandage becomes the Milky Way

Weeks later in deep space
In the French countryside
The figs and grapes are ripe

And the bandage becomes a kiss

You feed me figs
Your breath your lips the you I touch
Heals my slight imperfection

The bandage is a whisper in the leaves

Because of you
The little knife
Becomes an angel

A cloud of butterflies

Folding wings
In air which tastes
Of touching

South Wind

The wind
Dreams of Europa
Eros dreams of psyche

The oaks
Arc
Over the stone cottage

Two paths
Converge
In a field of sunflowers

With cows the colour
Of honey and cream
The colour of one stone room

Where the wind
Dreams
Of its wedding

Endless Knot

she woke up like an alphabet
the mannered rabbit of astrology
was watching from the shelf

the tree
a vase of wooden roses
the world

where the blackbird dreams
spoons of honey
in morning aureoles

the rings arrived from Penzance today
real myth and ornament
circles made of mist

two rings a formula
a tracery of vines
reflecting beauty

The *Tower Belle*
carries the wedding guests upriver
to where the birds are pure rain

sweet triangular rabbit
like a ceilidh on Cobham Ferry
whirls in whorls

the corn goddess hare
crop marks crossing stars
on the river of dawn

Queribus

watching Queribus while my lady sleeps
I dream of troubadours and troglodytes

the sky a blue flower
seen inside the stem

all the arches of the bridges bend
the air in veils of wild lavender

my lady dreams of elephants
gray tree trunks crossing moats

the Queen's conjuror
is a hot summer

high cloud island castles
songs and rocks

I dream a plume
of soft southern thistle